Minor Scale Studies for the Cello

Book Two

One-Octave Melodic Minor Scales (One-String)

by Cassia Harvey

A Minor: pages 1 - 10
E Minor: pages 11 - 20
C Minor: pages 21 - 30
E-flat Minor: pages 31 - 40

CHP102

©2004 by C. Harvey Publications All Rights Reserved.

www.charveypublications.com - print books
www.learnstrings.com - PDF downloadable books
www.harveystringarrangements.com - chamber music

Minor Scale Studies for the Cello

Book Two

One-Octave Melodic Minor Scales (One-String)

Practice Suggestions

1. Play with full bows and strong tone.

2. Use vibrato as much as possible.

3. Vary tempos and dynamics to be more expressive.

4. Shift at an even speed, with clear notes before and after each shift.

5. Crescendo to the top of each scale to build technique in the higher positions.

Minor Scale Studies for the Cello

Book Two

Cassia Harvey

A minor, First Fingering

Play this page entirely on the G string.

©2004 C. Harvey Publications® All Rights Reserved

Minor Scale Studies for the Cello, Book Two

Play this page entirely on the G string.

©2004 C. Harvey Publications® All Rights Reserved

A minor, Second Fingering

Play this page entirely on the G string.

©2004 C. Harvey Publications® All Rights Reserved

Play this page entirely on the G string.

A minor, Third Fingering

Play this page entirely on the G string.

©2004 C. Harvey Publications® All Rights Reserved

Minor Scale Studies for the Cello, Book Two

Play this page entirely on the G string.

©2004 C. Harvey Publications® All Rights Reserved

A minor, Fourth Fingering

Play this page entirely on the G string.

Play this page entirely on the G string.

A minor, Fifth Fingering

Play this page entirely on the G string.

©2004 C. Harvey Publications® All Rights Reserved

Minor Scale Studies for the Cello, Book Two
Play this page entirely on the G string.

E minor, First Fingering

Play this page entirely on the D string.

E minor, Second Fingering

Play this page entirely on the D string.

Minor Scale Studies for the Cello, Book Two

Play this page entirely on the D string.

E minor, Third Fingering

Play this page entirely on the D string.

Minor Scale Studies for the Cello, Book Two

Play this page entirely on the D string.

©2004 C. Harvey Publications® All Rights Reserved

E minor, Fourth Fingering

Play this page entirely on the D string.

Minor Scale Studies for the Cello, Book Two

Play this page entirely on the D string.

©2004 C. Harvey Publications® All Rights Reserved

E minor, Fifth Fingering

Play this page entirely on the D string.

Minor Scale Studies for the Cello, Book Two

Play this page entirely on the D string.

©2004 C. Harvey Publications® All Rights Reserved

C minor, First Fingering

Play this page entirely on the A string.

Minor Scale Studies for the Cello, Book Two

C minor, Second Fingering

Minor Scale Studies for the Cello, Book Two

C minor, Third Fingering

Minor Scale Studies for the Cello, Book Two

C minor, Fourth Fingering

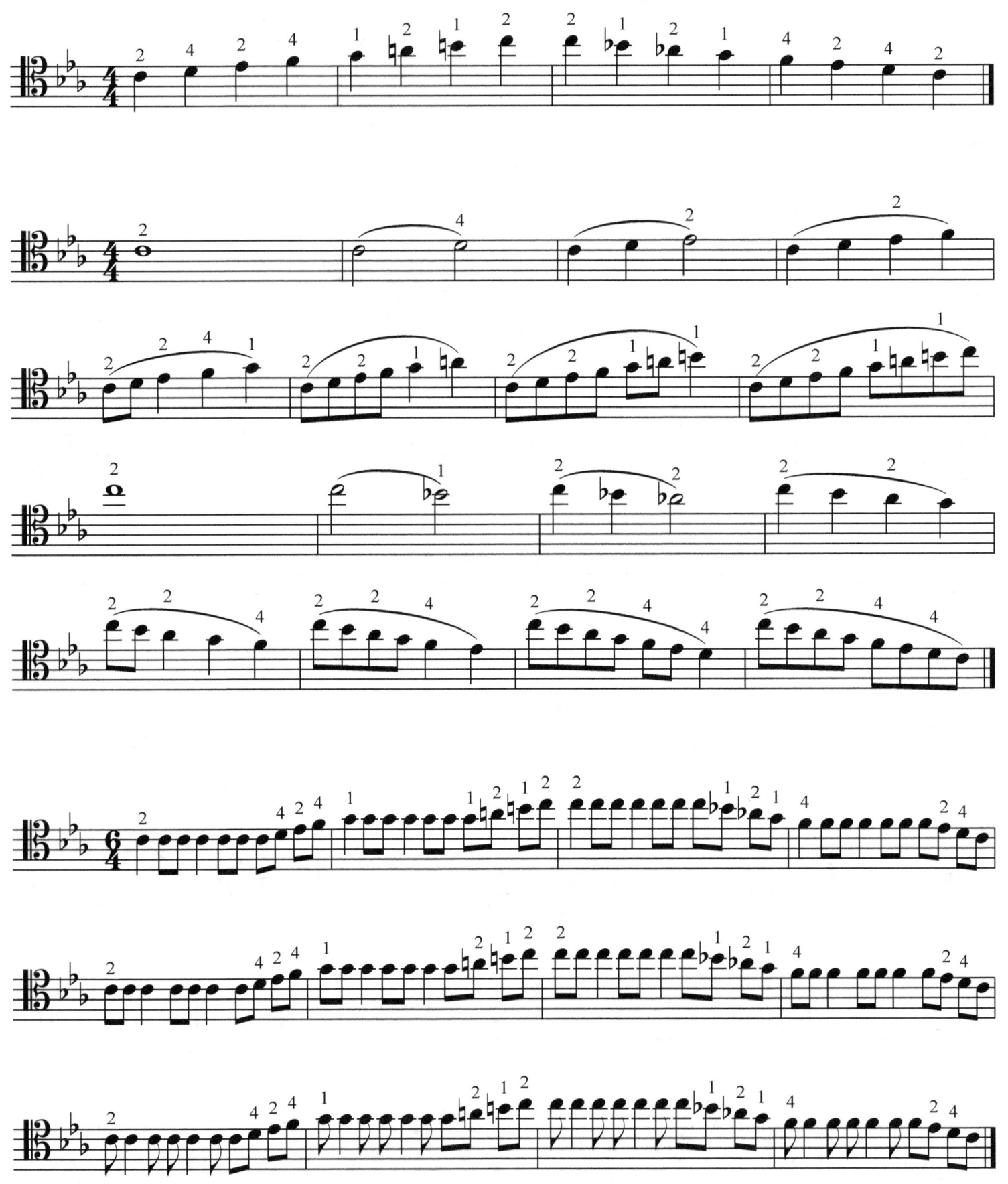

Minor Scale Studies for the Cello, Book Two

C minor, Fifth Fingering

Minor Scale Studies for the Cello, Book Two

32

Minor Scale Studies for the Cello, Book Two

E♭ minor, First Fingering

Play this page entirely on the C string.

©2004 C. Harvey Publications® All Rights Reserved

Minor Scale Studies for the Cello, Book Two

Play this page entirely on the C string.

Minor Scale Studies for the Cello, Book Two

Play this page entirely on the C string.

E♭ minor, Third Fingering

Play this page entirely on the C string.

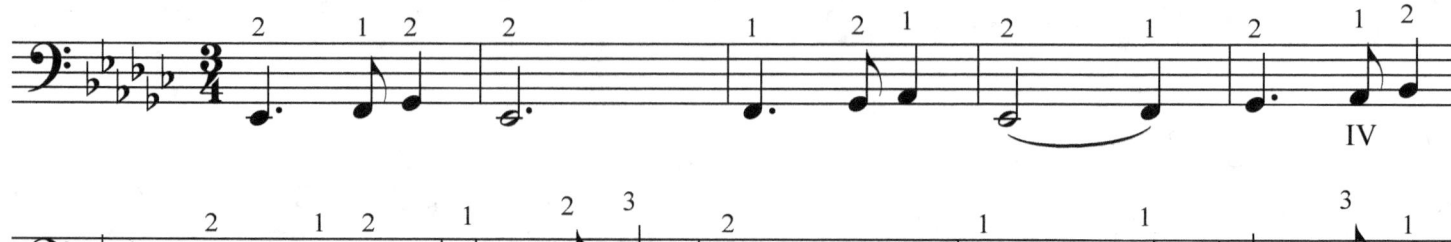

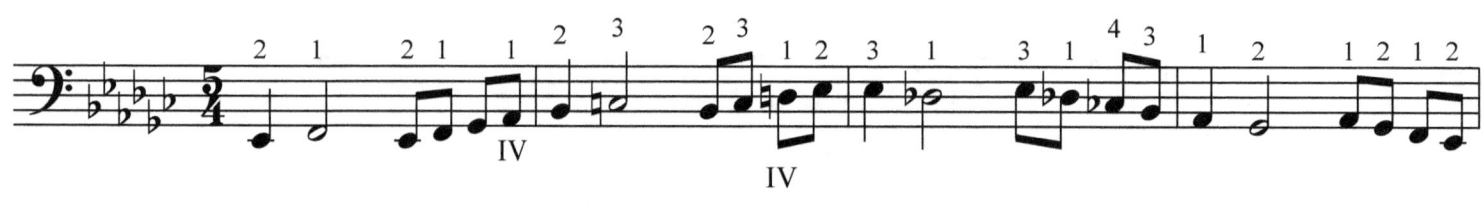

©2004 C. Harvey Publications® All Rights Reserved

Minor Scale Studies for the Cello, Book Two

Play this page entirely on the C string.

E♭ minor, Fourth Fingering

Play this page entirely on the C string.

Minor Scale Studies for the Cello, Book Two

Play this page entirely on the C string.

©2004 C. Harvey Publications® All Rights Reserved

Minor Scale Studies for the Cello, Book Two

Play this page entirely on the C string.

©2004 C. Harvey Publications® All Rights Reserved

Also available from www.charveypublications.com: CHP356
Learning Three-Octave Scales on the Cello

Part One: Learning the Major Scales

C Major Scale

Cassia Harvey

©2019 C. Harvey Publications All Rights Reserved.

www.ingramcontent.com/pod-product-compliance
Lightning Source LLC
Chambersburg PA
CBHW051426070526
44584CB00023B/3601